TRACKING A KILLER

Using Science to Solve Homicides

CHERITON
CHILDREN'S BOOKS

Published in 2023 by **Cheriton Children's Books**
1 Bank Drive West, Shrewsbury, Shropshire, SY3 9DJ, UK

© 2023 Cheriton Children's Books

First Edition

Author: Sarah Eason
Designer: Paul Myerscough
Editor: Louisa Simmons
Proofreader: Ella Hammond

Picture credits: Cover: Shutterstock/Andreiuc88; Inside: p1: Shutterstock/
Gorodenkoff; p4: Shutterstock/Matt Gush; p5: Shutterstock/Jack Dagley
Photography; p6: Shutterstock/Miljan Zivkovic; p7: Shutterstock/Microgen; p8:
Shutterstock/Maksim Shmeljov; p10: Shutterstock/Wulle; p11: Shutterstock/
Zoka74; pp12-13: Shutterstock/Macondo; p13: Shutterstock/Bits And Splits;
p14: Shutterstock/Massimo Todaro; p15: Shutterstock/Lukas Jonaitis; p16:
Shutterstock/Kevin L Chesson; p17: Shutterstock/Teresa Otto; p18: Shutterstock/
Gorodenkoff; p19: Shutterstock/Mehaniq; p20: Shutterstock/Nikkytok; pp22-23:
Shutterstock/adriaticfoto; p23: Shutterstock/Billion Photos; p24: Shutterstock/
Roxane 134; p25: Shutterstock/Couperfield; p26: Shutterstock/Carrastock; p28:
Shutterstock/Gorodenkoff; p29: Shutterstock/Jaroslav Noska; p30: Shutterstock/
Andrew Angelov; p31: Shutterstock/Kichigin; p33: Shutterstock/Xray Computer;
pp34-35: Shutterstock/9nong; p35: Shutterstock/Peter Porrini; p36: Shutterstock/
Motortion Films; p37: Shutterstock/GuruXOX; p38: Shutterstock/H_Ko; pp40-41:
Shutterstock/Alice-photo; p41: Shutterstock/Tsyklon; p42: Shutterstock/Maksim
Shmeljov; p43: Shutterstock/Kitreel; p44: Shutterstock/Andreiuc88.

Printed in China

Please visit our website,
www.cheritonchildrensbooks.com
to see more of our high-quality books.

CONTENTS

TRACKING A KILLER

Homicide is the killing of one person by another person. When the killing is deliberate, the crime is murder. Manslaughter is accidental or unintentional homicide, perhaps **committed** in self-defense or in a fight that got out of hand. Homicide is one of the most serious **offenses**—in some countries, certain types of murder carry the **death penalty**.

Murder Investigation

Two groups of people investigate homicide—the police and forensic scientists. The police interview **witnesses**, find out who the **victim** is, and try to **identify** and arrest the killer. The police need to prove that the arrested person is the killer. To do that, they must provide concrete **evidence**, and this is where **forensic** scientists can be critical in solving a case.

The United States has one of the highest rates of homicide in the developed world.

Knowing the Killer

Most victims know their killer, so the police usually look for a murderer among people known to the victim. Around one-fifth of homicide victims are women, of whom between around half and three-quarters are killed by a family member or their partner. If the police find a suspect at or near the crime scene, they are immediately arrested.

Most murders in the United States take place in the country's big cities.

USING SCIENCE TO SOLVE CRIMES

Scientists who specialize in crime are called forensic scientists. Their job is to find and examine evidence to help the police piece together what happened. They also help identify criminals. If a suspect is arrested, the forensic scientists' evidence may confirm whether or not they are the killer.

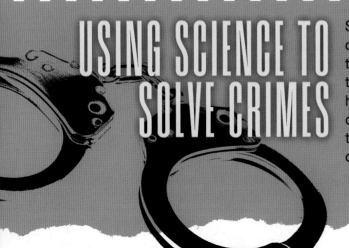

Evidence Experts

A body has been found, and the police are called to the scene of a possible murder—but how do they find the killer? First, they examine the body and check whether the killer is still at the scene, then they interview witnesses and start to figure out what happened. They also call in forensic scientists to collect evidence and **analyze** it in **microscopic** detail.

Handling the Body

The first person at the crime scene checks whether the victim is still breathing, and if they have a pulse. If the investigator is sure the victim is dead, they will try to establish the cause of death. If the person has been shot, stabbed, or hit with a heavy object, the investigators must search the crime-scene area to try and find the murder weapon.

At the Crime Scene

Even if a police officer is sure about the cause of death, the body must still be examined by a forensic scientist. The forensic scientist will then collect further evidence, such as **samples** of blood. Other forensic scientists photograph and record every piece of evidence collected.

When a forensic scientist arrives at a crime scene, they search the area.

3

4

LINE DO NOT CROSS

In the Lab

The evidence collected at the crime scene is taken to the police laboratory, or lab. There it is examined in detail. Any weapons are checked for fingerprints, and any samples of blood are carefully examined under a microscope.

Blood and other material collected at the crime scene are tested in the police laboratory.

CRIME SCIENCE

Police interview witnesses who may have seen the attack or something suspicious—for example, they may have seen the possible killer running away.

Evidence from witnesses can be extremely valuable, but must also be carefully examined—a crime can happen so quickly that witnesses can be mistaken.

The Crime Scene

The crime scene is the place at which the crime occurred. In a murder, this is often where the body is found. There may, however, be more than one crime scene, because the victim may have been attacked in one place and the body left or buried elsewhere. A murder investigation starts where the body is found.

No-Go Zone

As soon as the police arrive, one of the officers secures the crime scene. This may be part of the street or another outdoor area. It could also be a room, or even an entire building. The crime scene contains evidence that must not be lost or disturbed, so the whole scene is immediately sealed off, and the public are kept out.

CRIME SCIENCE

After the body has been examined and photographed, it is placed in a body bag and taken to the **autopsy** room. There, forensic **pathologists** examine it to find out more about the cause of death. They also try to figure out the time of death.

Forensic Search

When the forensic scientists arrive at a murder scene, they examine and photograph everything that may be connected to the killing. The photographs show exactly where each piece of evidence was found. Everything at a crime scene can be important. Murderers often leave clues without realizing it. They may leave footprints, fingerprints, or tiny threads from their clothes.

Essential Evidence

Every piece of evidence that is collected is placed in a separate, clean bag to make sure that it is not **contaminated** with blood or other evidence. For the same reason, crime scene investigators wear gloves and special clothes.

Forensic scientists examine every square inch of a crime scene, looking for evidence.

The Forensic Team

Forensic scientists collect and analyze evidence. Often, many different forensic specialists may be involved in solving a crime. There are two main groups: crime scene investigators who focus on different aspects of the crime scene, and others who work mainly in the crime lab.

Important Work

Crime scene investigators are responsible for identifying and collecting evidence at the crime scene. They include fingerprint specialists, photographers, and firearms specialists. All of the evidence collected at the crime scene is analyzed in the crime lab. Scientists in different departments within the lab concentrate on particular aspects of evidence, such as the body, blood, **deoxyribonucleic acid (DNA)**, bullets, and weapons. They use special equipment and scientific techniques to carry out their jobs.

Investigators mark out the position in which a body and any evidence was found to try to discover more about the cause of death.

10

A special light is used to detect fingerprints on any objects found at the crime scene.

Is It a Set Up?

Crime scene investigators have to be on the lookout for staged crime scenes. These are crime scenes that have been altered to make it look as if something other than the crime happened. For example, if a gun is put into the hand of a dead victim, a murder might be disguised as a **suicide**.

TRUE CRIME STORY

In the 1920s, Chicago was racked by battles between rival criminal gangs. One of the worst incidents occurred on Valentine's Day in 1929. Seven members of Bugs Moran's gang were gunned down by two men in police uniform.

The bullet casings were the same type as those used by the Chicago Police Department. Did the police shoot the gang? Forensic firearms expert Calvin Goddard tested every gun owned by the police department and was able to declare that none of them had been used in the **massacre**. Then, the search for the real gunmen began.

DIG FOR DATA

A database is a collection of information that is stored on a computer. It is organized so that any particular item can be easily found. Police departments keep information about criminals and crimes on databases. When a new crime is committed, they can search the databases for similarities to past crimes.

Kept on Record

For decades, the police have kept photographs of **convicted** criminals. They have also kept copies of their fingerprints. These are stored on police databases and can be easily accessed so that fingerprints found on a knife, for example, can be checked to see if they match fingerprints on the database. Today, the police record other identifying features, too.

Track and Trace

All vehicles carry a license plate. If the police know the license plate number of a vehicle seen near the killing, they can search a database to trace the number and the owner of the vehicle. Guns also have distinctive marks, which can be recorded and stored on a computer.

Criminal Style

Apart from identifying particular features about the killer, investigators study the way the crime was carried out. Murderers who have killed other victims often go about their crimes in a similar way. For example, they often use the same type of weapon and attack a similar type of victim in the same way. Using computers, investigators search for similarities with other attacks.

Crime Science

Forensic scientists are now able to analyze and identify far more evidence than they previously could. For example, they can now identify people through samples of blood. By reexamining evidence collected many years ago, they can sometimes crack previously unsolved cases.

Even small samples of blood can provide clues about homicides.

A WORLD OF INDIVIDUALS

Everyone in the world is unique. The billions of people in the world are all different in various ways that can be detected and recorded. Although identical twins look alike, they have unique differences, such as their fingerprint patterns. Police use these differences to help them identify people involved in a crime.

A New Look

It is possible for criminals to change their appearance. Many witnesses have only a fleeting glimpse of a killer and tend to remember things, such as clothes, which are very easy to change. For example, a different hairstyle or hair color quickly alters a person's appearance. For a man, shaving off or growing a beard changes the look of his face.

Teeth are one of the best markers for identifying a body.

Just like their teeth, everyone's fingerprints are unique.

Forensics and Features

Forensic scientists look for the features that a person cannot change. In particular, they examine the crime scene for fingerprints, blood, and traces of DNA. It is only in the last 40 years that forensic scientists have been able to test for DNA —the chemicals inside each **cell** which, among other things, determine how a person looks.

Revealed in Remains

Once a person is dead, their body begins to **decompose**. Although decomposed and very badly damaged bodies are more difficult to identify, many of their distinguishing features may remain. For example, teeth can last for centuries, so police can check the dental records of a missing person to see if they match the victim's teeth.

CRIME SCIENCE

Everybody has the same number of teeth, but everyone's teeth are slightly different in size and shape. Most people have one or two teeth that are not perfectly **aligned.** Other teeth may be chipped or missing. Dental records reveal all the details of a person's teeth and can be used to identify people.

Finding Fingerprints

The fine ridges on your fingertips help you feel surfaces and pick up small things. The ridges form a pattern of arches, loops, or whorls. Every finger has a different pattern, which stays the same throughout your life. That means that when you touch a hard, smooth surface, you leave behind a copy of your own unique patterns—your fingerprints.

Forensic Tools

At the crime scene, some fingerprints may be clearly visible, especially if they were made by someone with grease, dirt, or blood on their hands. Many others will not be visible. Forensic scientists use a very fine powder or special lights to reveal hidden prints. They examine likely surfaces, such as weapons, doors, and window frames. Once the prints are visible, they are photographed or lifted using a piece of **transparent** tape.

Perfect Prints

Doors and similar surfaces are covered with the fingerprints of many people. A lot of the prints will be smudged or partly covered by other prints. A crime scene investigator will try and find one or two clear prints. Digital cameras and computer **software** make this easier than it used to be. Today, investigators can sharpen up prints before they try to match them with known prints.

Forensic investigators check surfaces for any traces of prints.

TRUE CRIME STORY

As well as fingerprints, toe prints, ear prints, and palm prints are also unique. One of the most famous crimes solved using palm prints is the murder in 1963 of President John F. Kennedy, who was shot as he drove in an open car through Dallas, Texas. The shots came from a particular building, the Texas School Book Depository. When police searched the building they found a rifle with a palm print on it. It was matched to Lee Harvey Oswald, who was arrested for the crime.

The assassination of President John F. Kennedy and arrest of Oswald was reported by journalists around the world.

Useful Blood

Blood is extremely useful to forensic scientists. They take samples from the victim and look for bloodstains on walls, on the ground, on clothes, and on the weapon. Killers often try to get rid of bloodstains by washing or dumping the items, because they know they link them to a crime.

Checking with Chemicals

First, scientists test their samples to see whether the stains are in fact blood. Certain chemicals change color or glow when mixed with blood. For example, luminol glows when it reacts with even a tiny amount of blood. It can also detect blood on surfaces that have been cleaned or painted over.

Blood evidence can provide forensic scientists and crime investigators with important information about the crime.

8

The pattern of a bloodstain helps crime investigators **reconstruct** the crime. If the blood is spattered into many tiny drops, the investigators use string to trace each drop of blood back to the point where they all meet. This tells the investigators where the victim was when they were shot or hit.

Whose Blood?

Once the presence of human blood is confirmed, the scientists try to identify whose blood it is. There are four main blood groups—O, A, B, and AB. The blood group of each sample can be useful in distinguishing the victim's blood from other sources of blood. However, a blood-group match does not necessarily identify a particular person: only DNA can do that.

Clues in the Blood

The amount of blood at a crime scene also reveals information about the killing. Bleeding ceases as soon as a person's heart stops beating. A person who dies instantly sheds very little blood, so if only a small amount of blood is found at a crime scene, that suggests the person died quickly. A lot of blood, however, suggests that the victim was wounded for some time before they died.

Police search trash cans and other waste for abandoned clothes and weapons.

Liked by Evidence

Circumstantial evidence, such as footprints or threads of cloth, shows a possible link between a suspect and the crime scene. For example, if a footprint matches a shoe found at a suspect's home, it indicates that the suspect could have made it. Circumstantial evidence is not proof, however, because other people may also have the same type of shoe.

Tracked with a Tread

Shoes and tires both have **treads** to help them better grip the ground. Different types of shoes and tires have particular patterns of tread. Tread marks can link a suspect to a crime scene. If the ground is wet and muddy, investigators may find footprints indoors or tire prints outdoors. In addition, scientists may be able to match grains of mud or grit stuck in the treads to mud or grit at the crime scene.

Treads left at a crime scene can be vital evidence that can link a suspect with a crime.

A Trail of Threads

Cloth is woven from threads of cotton, wool, or **synthetic material**. The threads are made up of many tiny strands twisted together. When cloth is rubbed—during a struggle, for example—some of the strands may cling to the victim. Using a special microscope, scientists can compare fibers found at the crime scene with **fibers** from the suspect's clothes. If they match, the suspect could be the killer.

CRIME SCIENCE

Unfortunately, matching fibers found at a crime scene to a killer is not a perfect science. Recent research has shown that fibers can drift in the air from one person to another, which is called "contactless airborne transfer." This means that a perfectly innocent person could be near a crime scene, and fibers from a victim could travel through the air and land on them. That could link the innocent person with a crime they never committed.

21

SEARCH FOR DNA

Your body is made up of trillions of tiny cells. Different types of cells make up your skin, for example, or your heart, but every cell contains the same DNA, and each person's DNA is different. For that reason, being able to match DNA to a particular person has made identifying criminals much easier.

DNA Signs

Wherever you go and whatever you touch, you leave behind a trace of DNA. Whole hairs and flakes of skin fall from your body. Body fluids, particularly blood, saliva (or spit), and sweat, all contain DNA. Crime scene investigators look at everything for traces of DNA, then collect it. Investigators have to be extremely careful when collecting samples. Just a few cells contain enough DNA to identify an individual, but only if the sample has been correctly stored and preserved. They have to make sure that the sample is not contaminated by their own DNA, or by other evidence from the crime scene or the lab.

Making a Match

At the lab, forensic scientists analyze the DNA sample. First, they extract the DNA from the sample collected by crime scene investigators. They do this to make sure that they are testing the DNA alone. For example, if the sample collected from a crime scene is a piece of fabric, it is important to separate the DNA molecules from clothing molecules, which could later affect the testing stage if they are still present.

Scientists also check to make sure that DNA is human before testing it, and does not belong to another organism, such as bacteria. Once it has been determined that the DNA is human, copies of it are made. This is to ensure that scientists have enough good-quality DNA samples to carry out their tests.

Each DNA sample is analyzed and then turned into a pattern of gray bands, which are printed out. Scientists then compare the patterns from two samples to see if they match. They may compare DNA collected at the crime scene with DNA in a database, or they may compare it with a fresh sample from a suspect.

Crime Science

In the past, many samples of DNA were too small to analyze and were therefore never used. Today, if only a small DNA sample can be found, scientists now copy it and **replicate** it to provide them with a much larger sample with which to work.

This image shows the structure of DNA.

TOOLS FOR KILLING

Some murderers kill with their hands or feet, but most use a weapon. Weapons include guns and switchblades, which are designed to harm people, but everyday objects can also be turned into **lethal** weapons. Kitchen knives, baseball bats, and many other types of objects can become murder weapons.

Finding the Weapon

Finding the weapon is a crucial step toward finding the killer. Sometimes, a weapon is found at the crime scene, but not usually. Many killers try to get rid of the weapon to avoid being caught with it. They may drop it close to the crime scene as they run away, or they may throw it in a river or lake. They may even try to wipe it clean of fingerprints and throw it in a trash can.

Police divers search for missing weapons at the bottom of rivers, lakes, and ponds.

When a Weapon Cannot Be Found

Even if the weapon is missing, clues about it may be left at the crime scene. When a gun is used, a shell case often drops to the ground when a bullet is fired. Since different types of gun use different cartridges, the shell case and the bullets can indicate the type of gun used. Guns are the most common murder weapons

Sometimes, a gun is found at a crime scene and collected as evidence. If the gun cannot be found, cartridges, or empty shells, give vital clues to the type of gun used to fire them.

in the United States, probably because they kill quickly and can be used from a distance. They account for around twice as many deaths as all the other weapons put together.

CRIME SCIENCE

A pathologist can learn a great deal about a weapon from the victim's wounds. For example, a bullet may enter the body and become lodged, or it may leave the body through an exit hole, indicating the size and shape of the bullet used. The shape of a knife wound can indicate the size and type of knife used.

Killings with Guns

There are two main types of gun —handguns and rifles. Handguns are small enough to conceal on the body and can be fired with one hand. They include revolvers and pistols, and account for around three-quarters of **fatal** shootings. Rifles are larger and have a long **barrel**, so are more accurate if used from a distance.

TRUE CRIME STORY

John Branion, a doctor in Chicago, discovered his wife's dead body, which had been shot several times. A forensic scientist examined the shell cases and bullets and said that they came from a Walther PPK. Branion claimed that he did not own such a gun. When police searched his home, however, they found ammunition for a Walther PPK and references to a gun with a particular **serial number**. They traced the serial number and found it was from a Walther PPK that had been given to Branion as a present. Branion was convicted of the murder.

Understanding Guns

When a gunman pulls the trigger of a gun, a bullet is released. It spins at high speed toward the target. The bullet is loaded into the gun in a **cartridge**, which contains gunpowder. Pulling the trigger ignites the gunpowder so that it explodes, and forces the bullet down the gun's barrel. The empty cartridge falls to the ground.

A Smoking Gun?

When a gun is fired, most of the gases and particles from the explosion escape down the barrel. This has given rise to the idea of "a smoking gun." Although the gases disappear in an instant, they often leak out, spraying a powder, called gunshot **residue**, over the killer and the surroundings.

Many police departments and crime investigation units have shooting galleries. Investigators study guns as they are used, then apply what they have learned when investigating gun crimes.

Digging Deeper

Police do not only want to prove that a particular suspect is the killer, they also want to figure out exactly how the killing took place, and how many people were involved.

Clues on the Body

Gunshot wounds on the victim's body can reveal a lot of information. For example, if gunshot residue is found around the bullet wound, it shows that the killer was fewer than 2 feet (0.6 m) from the victim when the gun was fired. By looking at the entry wound and the exit wound, if there is one, a firearms expert can calculate the angle at which the bullet entered the body.

Tracking the Bullet

A bullet may ricochet, or bounce, off a wall or furniture before or after hitting the victim. Crime scene investigators look for nicks in furniture and dents in walls to help them reconstruct the path of the bullet. They may use string to trace the path of the bullet back from the body to figure out where the gunman was standing.

The position in which bullets are found provides important information about a crime.

Tracing the path of the bullet helps investigators learn if a killer fired several shots from one position, or the gunman or the victim moved during the attack. There may have been more than one gunman, or the killer may have used more than one gun.

Analyzing Bullets

Most guns are designed to make the bullet spin as it moves through the air. Spinning keeps the bullet moving straight along its path.

The bullet is spun by a spiral of grooves cut into the inside of the barrel of the gun. The grooves scratch the bullet, leaving what is known as rifling marks. Each machine in a gun factory makes a particular pattern of grooves, so each type of gun has a distinctive rifling pattern. The gun-making machine also wears as it is used, changing the grooves in each new gun. That means the rifling marks produced by each gun are different, so a bullet can be identified with a particular gun.

CRIME SCIENCE

Even if the crime scene investigators do not find any weapons, they collect all the bullets and shell casings that they find. These not only tell them how many guns were used, but also help them reconstruct the crime. An investigator then recreates the crime scene, showing exactly how the body and the empty shell cases were found.

Pathologists Explain

Scientists can't identify a particular knife or another sharp **implement**, such as a screwdriver, as the murder weapon unless the victim's blood is found on it. If no blood is found on weapons, investigators rely on pathologists for information revealed by the wounds on the body to help them reconstruct what happened.

When a Victim Is Stabbed

The type of wound that is inflicted depends on how a weapon is used. Sharp blades, such as knives, are often used to stab a victim. A stab wound is usually as wide as the blade, and can go deep into the victim's body. A deep cut is likely to damage a **vital organ**, such as the heart, lungs, or liver, or may cut an **artery**. A killer may stab a victim several times before leaving them to bleed to death.

Weapons are always photographed at the crime scene before being transported to the lab for further forensic investigation.

CRIME SCIENCE

An autopsy describes every wound found on the body. The depth of a wound shows how the weapon was wielded. The angle of a stab wound helps forensic scientists figure out where the killer was in relation to the victim—for example, whether the attacker stood in front, behind, or above the victim.

Autopsies are always carried out in sterile environments to avoid contaminating the evidence.

Clues in the Cuts

Knives are also used to cut across the skin. A cut across the throat is almost certainly an attempt to murder the victim, but the body may have other cuts, too. If the victim tried to fight off the attacker, their hands and arms may have cuts. If the body shows a deep, wedge-shaped wound, it could mean that the killer used an ax or similar heavy chopping weapon.

Blows, Breaks, and Bleeds

Murderers sometimes kill their victims with a blunt implement, such as a baseball bat or another heavy object. Blows to the body produce visible bruising and can also cause lethal bleeding inside the body. Heavy blows may break bones. It is the pathologist's job to examine the body and figure out how the injuries were caused.

Deadly Damage

Heavy blows can damage vital organs. Many organs, such as the liver, contain large amounts of blood, which escapes inside the body and can cause death. When a pathologist examines the inside of a body, they look for internal bruising and bleeding.

Broken Bones

Battering someone with a blunt implement can break or crush a bone. The type of injury and the direction of the break can help the pathologist decide how the break occurred. For example, if the victim's head was battered, their skull may be cracked or shattered, fatally damaging the brain.

Battered and Bruised

When something smashes against flesh, it breaks tiny blood vessels below the surface. The blood leaks out and causes a bruise. Pathologists look at the shape of the bruise to see if they can tell what made it—was the victim stamped on, for example, or maybe they were hit by a car?

CRIME SCIENCE

A pathologist examines bruises to see whether they formed before, during, or after the murder. Old bruises need to be identified and possibly excluded from a murder investigation. It is easy to identify a bruise made after the person has died, because the bruise will have bled less and be a light-brown color.

The amount of damage inflicted by a blunt implement depends on the angle and force of the blow. Pathologists will examine X-rays, along with looking at a body itself, to try to determine the cause of death.

PINPOINT POISON

Not all murders occur instantly. A poison is a substance that kills a person when it is **ingested** —sometimes hours after it enters their body. Poisoning is a very old method of murdering a person, and is much rarer than other forms of homicide. The most common way of administering a poison is to mix it into food or drink.

Old and Deadly

Traditional poisons include arsenic and cyanide, but today, rat poison, morphine, and antifreeze are common, too. Arsenic has no taste and is difficult to detect in food. It can kill within a few hours, days, or even weeks.

Who Is Responsible?

A poisoner must have access to their victim, so often family members are immediate suspects in cases of poisoning. Doctors and other medical staff may also be suspects, because they have access to dangerous drugs. If several people die unexpectedly in the hospital, the hospital's staff may be suspected. A recent famous case of hospital poisoning is one involving nurse Charles Cullen. When a number of patients began to die under his care, alarm bells rang. Cullen was investigated and eventually arrested for killing his patients by giving them fatal doses of drugs while he was supposed to be caring for them. All Cullen's victims were discovered to have abnormally high amounts of deadly drugs in their bodies. The nurse confessed to killing 40 of his patients, but the true number is believed to be far greater.

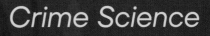

Crime Science

A toxicologist is an expert in poisons who is called in when poisoning is suspected. Toxicologists look for traces of a poison in the body. They examine the contents of the stomach, the liver, blood, and urine. If the poison is no longer in the body, they look for damage to the body caused by the poison.

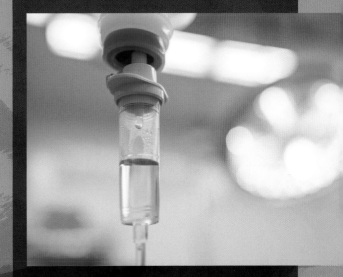

In a hospital setting, poison might be administered to patients via an intravenous (IV) drip, like this one.

CHAPTER 4

MURDER MANHUNT

The priority for police investigating a homicide is to identify and find the killer or killers. Deliberate, planned murders may have no witnesses. Gang killings, on the other hand, may have several, but the witnesses may be too scared to give evidence.

Talking to Witnesses

Police interview witnesses to find out what they saw. Did they, for example, get a clear look at the killer, or did they notice the color and make of a getaway car, or even the license plate number? If the killing happened in a public place, such as a store, gas station, or street, it may have been recorded on closed-circuit television (CCTV). Killers, however, are often aware of cameras and hide their faces.

Investigating with an Image

The task of finding a killer is much easier if the police have a good image of them. Scientists use all the information available to produce a likeness, which is then circulated to the police and may be published in newspapers or on television.

As well as documenting evidence at a crime scene, investigators will search for any nearby CCTV cameras that could provide them with more clues about the killer.

Links to a Killer

Involving the public can produce vital evidence and links to a killer. People who did not witness the homicide may have other information that is useful in tracking down the murderer. Police sometimes appeal to the public through television shows. The television company reconstructs the crime, and asks for any relevant information. The reconstruction may jog someone's memory and help find a suspect.

Reconstructions shown on television can draw attention to a crime and help find witnesses.

CRIME SCIENCE

Crime investigators work with television organizations to try and find killers. Crime television shows invite viewers to phone in with information. Often, several people call in with information about the same person. The information may be anonymous, but it can provide just the lead the police need to finally crack the case.

Wanted for Murder

Getting a good, clear image of a suspect is critical for the police. If the suspect has been convicted for previous crimes, the police will have a photograph on their database. There may also be a good image captured on a CCTV camera. If an image of a suspect does not already exist, one has to be created.

Identity Kits

The technology for producing a good likeness has improved enormously in the last 60 years. In the past, an artist drew a portrait of a wanted person, based on witnesses' accounts. Then, in 1959, a Los Angeles policeman invented Identikit. It was a bank of ready-made drawings of different features, such as the mouth, eyes, and nose, from which a witness could choose. Today, photographed features are adjusted on a computer to create an E-fit.

The iris is the colored part of the eye around the pupil. Everyone's irises are different and cannot be changed. They are important clues that can help link a killer with a crime.

Into the Future

In some cases a person may be wanted 20 or more years after the only available photographs were taken. Unsolved cases, called cold cases, are never forgotten. Using a computer, an expert can use a past photo to produce a new image of what the person is likely to look like several decades later.

Changing to Hide

To avoid being identified, people on the run may go to great lengths to disguise their appearance. As well as changing the color and cut of their hair, some even resort to using plastic surgery to change their features. They may, for example, change the shape of their nose to alter their face.

CRIME SCIENCE

Forensic scientists have worked with computer specialists to produce software that can help identify the same person before and after their plastic surgery. The program matches individual features, instead of attempting to match the whole face.

CATCH ON CAMERA

Killers and other criminals are more likely to be caught on camera than ever before. Surveillance cameras watch public places both inside and out. Smartphones take instant photos. These cameras can deter attacks, but they are also useful in identifying and tracking people and cars after a criminal event.

Camera Control

Surveillance cameras are video cameras linked to a central control room. The cameras may be watched by a guard or police officer, but they can also be **monitored** or scanned by a computer. This makes it much easier and faster to identify particular people or suspicious behavior. In recent years, the quality of the pictures recorded by surveillance cameras has become much clearer.

Traffic Tracking

Traffic cameras monitor streets and roads. They photograph speeding vehicles and vehicles committing other traffic offenses. Traffic cameras can also be linked to a database of license plate numbers. This allows police to search for and track a getaway car or a car that was seen near a crime scene.

Crime Science

Cell phone cameras have changed modern-day policing. They are very easy to use, take instant, good-quality photographs, and most people keep their phones on hand and can use them to record crimes. Some people even record crimes or criminals accidentally, when they are photographing something else. The evidence can be used by crime investigators to track down homicide suspects.

A surveillance camera on the side of a building records everyone who passes by. CCTV is now a vital tool in the hunt for homicide perpetrators.

THE FUTURE OF TRACKING KILLERS

Forensic scientists are developing better ways to catch killers. Modern computer software and databases store and monitor more data than ever, which can be used to link crimes with perpetrators.

Changing the Law

In the United States, the details of guns used in crimes are stored on a nationwide database. Since any gun can be identified from its unique rifling marks, changing the law so that all guns have to be registered when they are sold would make it easier to trace gun crimes to the perpetrators who committed them.

Tracking Traces

Wherever a person goes and whatever they touch, they leave behind traces of DNA. However, forensic scientists can now track people without having to find physical evidence. For example, when people travel by car, the license plate is recorded on traffic cameras. Calls made on a cell phone can be easily traced, as can transactions made with a bank card. Wherever a person goes, a digital record is left behind.

Forensic investigation is critical in helping solve homicides.

DNA Databases?

As detecting and analyzing DNA becomes more reliable, a central database of everyone's DNA could be set up. Forensic scientists would then be able to instantly identify anyone whose DNA is found at a crime scene.

People are concerned, however, that such a database would invade privacy. Most people do agree though that if scientific developments can help stop or solve crimes, investing in crime science must be an essential part of our crime investigation future.

MAKE CRIME SCIENCE YOUR FUTURE

Working in forensic investigation requires sharp thinking and hard work. Investigators must explore every detail as they examine crimes, and follow every avenue to track down a **suspect**. If you think you have what it takes to work in this cutting-edge science field, overleaf you'll find a career guide that could one day help you track down a killer.

CRIME-STOPPING CAREERS

COULD YOU TRACK A KILLER?

Crime dramas win record viewings, and these gripping shows have inspired many to enter the world of crime science and investigation. It is an amazingly exciting field to work in, with new, game-changing developments emerging all the time.

However, crime dramas don't always show the differences between roles in crime science and investigation. It is important to distinguish between the work of a forensic scientist and a crime scene investigator before making decisions about what type of job you might enjoy. The below charts explain the differences.

Forensic Scientist

Workplace: Most forensic scientists work in laboratories, where they analyze the evidence gathered by crime scene investigators.

Tools used: Forensic scientists use lab-based tools such as microscopes, spectrometry machines, and toxicology tools to carry out work.

Scope of work: It is possible to specialize in many different areas, from ballistics and fingerprint analysis through toxicology and DNA analysis.

Crime Scene Investigator

Workplace: Crime scene investigators go to crime scenes and collect evidence. They also analyze any evidence gathered at the crime scene.

Tools used: Crime scene investigators use in-the-field tools such as cameras, adhesive tapes, tweezers, collection bags, flashlights, blood-collection kits, and place cards.

Scope of work: Compared with a forensic scientist, the scope of this role is far narrower, but crime scene investigators could move on to other investigative fields, such as working for private investigation companies.

To pursue a career in forensic science or crime scene investigation, follow this simple flowchart.

Focus on your science subjects at school	Working in forensic science requires a strong scientific background, so concentrating on science topics at school is a must.
After school, earn an associate degree	Earning an associate degree applies to both forensic scientists and crime scene investigators, although some crime scene investigators enter the job without a degree, for example, they move into the work through the police force. After the degree stage, crime scene investigators will move into a job post. A forensic scientist will need to move on to further qualifications.
Earn a bachelor's degree	A forensic scientist will need a bachelor's degree for entry-level jobs. Often, employers will also ask for a master's degree too.
Choose a career area	At degree stage, forensic science students decide what area to specialize in, such as ballistics or autopsies, and complete courses that focus on those areas.
Apply for jobs	Once in a suitable role, valuable on-the-job training will be gained.

GLOSSARY

aligned brought into line

analyze to carefully study something in order to better understand it

artery a vessel that carries blood from the heart through the body

autopsy an examination of a body after death to determine the cause of death

barrel the part of a gun down which the bullet travels after it is fired

cartridge a container that holds a bullet and powder

cell the smallest part of all living things

circumstantial evidence evidence that shows a person could have been involved in a crime but does not prove that they were involved

committed carried out

contaminated made dirty or changed by coming into contact with a substance

convicted found guilty of a crime and put in prison for that crime

database a usually large collection of data organized especially for quick search and retrieval of information

death penalty the punishment of death given by a court of law for very serious crimes, such as homicide

decompose to rot, or break down, into smaller parts

deoxyribonucleic acid (DNA) the unique code inside every human body cell that controls every element of how we look

evidence information, objects, or substances that are related to a crime

fatal resulting in death

fibers small pieces of cloth

forensic applying scientific knowledge to solve criminal and legal problems

identify to figure out who someone is

implement a tool

ingested taken into the body through the digestive system

lethal resulting in death

massacre the killing of a large number of people

microscopic describes something that is so small it can only be seen with the aid of a microscope

monitored checked or kept watch over

offenses criminal acts

pathologists doctors who examine bodies to determine the causes of death

perpetrators people who carry out acts

reconstruct to rebuild a chain of events

replicate to copy

residue parts left behind after something is removed

samples small parts of something taken to examine them scientifically

serial number a number indicating an object's place in a series and used as a means of identification of that object

software computer programs that tell a computer what to do

suicide the act or an instance of taking one's own life

suspect a person suspected of carrying out a crime

synthetic material a man-made material

transparent fine or sheer enough to be seen through

treads the grooves cut into tires or the soles of shoes

victim a person who has been injured, harmed, or killed by another person

vital organ a body part that is essential for life, such as the heart or brain

witnesses people who saw something, such as a crime, take place

FIND OUT MORE

Books

Cooper, Chris. *Forensic Science: Discover the Fascinating Methods Scientists Use to Solve Crimes* (DK Eyewitness). DK Children, 2020.

Kortuem, Amy. *Blood Evidence* (Crime Solvers). Capstone Publishing, 2019.

Newquist, H.P. *Scene of the Crime: Tracking Down Criminals With Forensic Science*. Viking Books for Young Readers, 2021.

Websites

Learn more about crime science at:
www.explainthatstuff.com/forensicscience.html

Find out what happens at a crime scene investigation at:
www.howstuffworks.com/csi.htm

Find out more about DNA and how it works at:
https://kids.britannica.com/kids/article/DNA/390730

Publisher's note to educators and parents:
All the websites featured above have been carefully reviewed to ensure that they are suitable for students. However, many websites change often, and we cannot guarantee that a site's future contents will continue to meet our high standards of educational value. Please be advised that students should be closely monitored whenever they access the Internet.

INDEX

About the Author

Sarah Eason is an experienced children's book author who has written many science books for children. She loves watching crime-detective shows, and after researching and writing this book is more fascinated than ever by the world of homicide investigation and forensic science.